HOW TO MAKE SLIME

A DIY Beginner's Guide to Creating and Making Your Own Slime Step-By-Step

Table of Contents

Introduction

What is slime, you ask? It's more than just stretchy goo. It's science. It's a learning opportunity for adults and children alike. When thinking about the science behind slime, you need to look at the ingredients. Slime needs the right kind of glue and an activator. The best glue has a PVA (polyvinal acetate), like simple school glue. For the activator, you need something from the boron family. This can be anything from contact solution or liquid starch to borax powder. When these two ingredients are mixed together, you get cross-linking. Chemistry!

Slime is an application of chemistry. It involves states of matter - liquids, solids, and gases - and when they are put together, you get to see how they all act under various conditions. Slime is not a solid or a liquid and does not have its own shape; it will fill whatever space it is placed in. Because it is elastic, it can bounce like a ball. It also pulls very nicely, unless pulled too fast. If the slime is pulled apart too fast, the chemical bonds will break and it will fall apart.

Once the chemical bonds are formed from mixing the PVA glue and the activator together, a new substance is formed. This cross-linking changes the viscosity of the substance and the molecules become tangled together to create slime.

Slime Basics

Slime is for everyone, not just kids. Not only is it fun, it's also educational. There are so many different slime recipes out there that you'll never get bored! And the best part is that they all follow a similar structure. This is great if you want to make different types of slime, because you don't have to get too many new ingredients. The ingredients can be interchangeable as well. However, once you start getting to the more advanced slimes, you might need to invest in some new ingredients.

You will also come to find that slime has a mind of its own. Sometimes measuring out the ingredients works out great. Other times, you need to improvise and play around to get your desired consistency.

Advantages of Making Your Own Slime

You can buy slime or slime kits almost anywhere these days. However, there are many advantages to making your own. Not only is it fun to make the slime, you'll also save money, use the ingredients you want, and learn about science in the process.

- **All about the science.** Slime can be very educational for children. It not only teaches them about measurements, it also teaches them about the science of combining ingredients to create a new product with a new consistency.

- **Saving money.** Not only is it cheaper to make your own slime, you will also have the ingredients around to make more batches. You can make as much or as little as you want. And since slime doesn't last very long, it's nice to have the option to try new slimes and make more whenever you like.

- **Customizing your slime.** When purchasing the slime kits, they only provide you with one way to make the slime. When you buy the ingredients separately, you insure that you get the ingredients that best suit you and your needs, and you make it your own. You get to customize the style, color, and type of slime you want.

- **Scented slime.** Adding scents to your slime can help you relax and cope with anxiety and stress, or you can just enjoy smelling it.

Kinds of Slime

There is a wide variety of slimes to choose from. Which kind you want to make will depend on your time, the materials you have or want to purchase, and if you want to do something basic or more advanced.

- **Basic slime.** These are the slime recipes that call for simple ingredients and are the easiest to make. The ingredients consist of glues (white, clear, glitter) and contact solution or borax. There are other variations, but these are your key glues and activators. Basic slime does not mean simple white boring slime; you can add food coloring or glitter as well. Just keep it simple.

- **More advanced slime.** These are the slimes that use ingredients that you will find in craft stores or online. They include foam beads, magnetic powders, and more specialized ingredients.

- **Scented slime.** These are somewhat advanced slimes. You will need special ingredients and/or essential oils for these. You can find these at grocery stores or online; they are not very expensive or hard to find.

- **Slime-like products.** There are products that you can make that are like slime, but have different properties. These include oobleck, playdough, and silly putty.

Getting Ready: Supplies and Equipment

Making slime is a science, and even when following the instructions, things can turn out differently than you had planned. Even with the simple materials and ingredients, you might need to improvise depending on which slime you are making and how your ingredients are working with each other.

Materials

The materials you need to make slime are quite simple and do not change, no matter what type of slime you are making. All of these materials can be found in your kitchen or bought at a local grocery store.

Mixing bowl: You can use any mixing bowl you have, but using a glass one is the easiest. Just make sure it has enough room for the ingredients and mixing.

Measuring cups: You will need all sizes of measuring cups to make your slime. You will be using the 1 cup, ½ cup, 1/3 cup, and ¼ cup.

Measuring spoons: It is always handy to have your measuring spoons with you. You will use them as often as you use the measuring cups. You will need the 1 tablespoon, ½ tablespoon, 1 teaspoon, and the ½ teaspoon.

Something to mix with: Mixing and kneading are inevitable when making slime so having something to mix with is key. A spoon, craft stick, or anything else you have lying around will be fine. Then make sure you have your hands ready! Kneading and playing with your slime is how you make sure that you have the right consistency, that it is not too sticky to play with, and that all of your ingredients are properly mixed together.

Airtight container or Ziploc bags: Storing slime properly is important if you want to be able to play with it again. This means that you must have an airtight container. Ziploc bags work the best, but other containers will work as well. These do not have to be large bags, just big enough to store your slime.

Clean surface: When you knead or even play with your slime, you will need a clean surface. If dust gets into your slime it will take some of the stick away. You also do not want to get your slime stuck to a surface which will be hard to clean.

Ingredients

A lot of the ingredients from one slime recipe to another are the same or similar. All of the ingredients can be purchased at your local grocery store. However, you might need to purchase some special ingredients online or at a craft store. Listed below are the main ingredients you should keep on hand for making slime.

Glue: It does not matter which brand you use. Elmer's is the most well-known brand, but any will do. You also have to choose between white or clear glue depending on what color you want the outcome to be or whatever you have on hand.

Baking soda: If you have this at home, use what you have. Otherwise buy a small box.

Water: Tap water works just fine. You do not need any special type of water.

Contact lens solution: When buying contact solution, make sure it contains boric acid and sodium borate. The brand does not matter as long as it contains the correct ingredients.

Food coloring: Using the main colors for your slime works great! Those are colors that can be made into a variety of other colors as well. If you use white glue, your colors may come out more pastel looking, depending on the number of drops you add in.

Shaving cream: Make sure you do not confuse shaving cream with shaving gel. The gel will not work for making slime. The shaving cream can be any kind you want or have on hand.

Liquid starch: You can find this at many grocery stores in the cleaning aisle. If not, you can order it online in bulk.

Extra additives: These include glitter, foam, iron, essential oils, Jell-O, sand, clay, fishbowl beads, and much more.

Instructions

Since making slime is a science, it does require some skills, but nothing too extensive. The various types of slime are made using different processes, but this section will focus on the process of making two of the basic slimes: foam slime and glitter slime.

Preparing the Things You Need

The first thing you need to do is gather everything you will need for your slime, including your measuring cups, measuring spoons and mixing bowl. It is important to have everything set out on your counter for easy access, so you can work without interruption. These are the basic ingredients you will need:

For the fluffy slime:

- Elmer's white glue

- Baking soda

- Water

- Shaving cream (not shaving gel)

- Contact solution

- Food coloring (to your preference)

- Stir stick (a thick craft stick)

The Process of Making Fluffy Slime

The process of making slime is chemistry; however, it is not rocket science. The ingredients need to be fairly precise, but there is always going to be some leeway. Every step in the process is important and has a purpose. We need an activator and a reactor. Below are the general steps for making fluffy slime:

1. Measure out all of your ingredients.

To make the process go easier and faster, it is best to measure out all of your ingredients so that you have them ready when you need to use them. This makes it more difficult to forget a step or an ingredient.

2. Pour your glue into the mixing bowl and then mix in your baking soda.

3. Add your water and stir until it is all mixed together. It will still look watery, but that is okay since some of the water will separate and rise to the top.

4. Then add your shaving cream and mix completely. This might take a little elbow grease. Your liquids will not want to mix well with the shaving cream at first, but keep mixing and they will blend together nicely. Once mixed, you can add your food coloring and stir some more until you reach your desired color.

5. Once you have your desired color, you can add in your contact solution. Be careful not to add too much, otherwise the slime will become hard and will not stretch like you want it to.

6. Now you need to start mixing the contact solution in. Once it becomes too hard to stir and pulls away from the edges of the bowl you can start kneading the mixture with your hands.

7. Then you will get the final product. It will look thicker and less like normal slime, but that's okay, because it's the fluffy slime and has shaving cream in it. It will still pull apart and act like regular slime.

Process of Making Glitter Slime

This process is slightly different than with your fluffy slime. To make glitter slime requires fewer steps and has completely different results.

1. To start, once again we are going to add our glue to our mixing bowl and then add in our baking soda. Stir it in really well.

2. Next we will add in our glitter. You can use as much or as little as you like. However, the more you put in, the more it will shine through. You will then need to mix it all in.

3. Now you can choose the color of your slime and put your food coloring in. Then mix it up really well.

4. Now it is time for the contact solution. This will activate the slime and give it the viscosity that we want. Once you stir it all in it will start to pull away from the edges of the bowl, like so. This is when you have to start kneading with your hands. This is an important step. The slime might still be extremely sticky, but just add in a little more contact solution. You need to knead it with your hands to ensure that all of the ingredients are mixed thoroughly.

5. Now that you have kneaded your slime, PLAY AWAY!

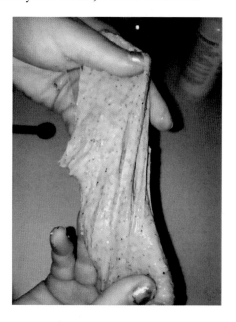

Proper Storage

Make sure to store your slime in an airtight container or Ziploc bag that is not too big. If it is too big, there will be unnecessary extra space and more ways for air to seep in. For some of the recipes, you should store your slime in the refrigerator or freezer. This will keep it fresh and make it easier for you to play with over and over again.

Tips and Tricks

The tips and tricks for making your slime are contained within each individual recipe. They are clearly noted and or marked with **. These tips and tricks may vary depending on products, measurements, and much more, so do what is best for you and your slime. Do not rush through making it, take it slow, and have fun. DO NOT STRESS about your recipes! These are meant to be fun and help you relax.

Recipes

The best thing about making your own slime is all the ways you can customize it to your wants and needs. You can even customize these slime recipes by adding or taking out certain ingredients. Just make sure that you have your PVA and your activator.

Basic Slime Recipes

Fluffy Slime

Ingredients:

Option 1

- ½ teaspoon baking soda
- Food coloring
- ¼ cup water
- 2 cups shaving cream
- 2/3 cup white glue

Option 2

- 1/2 cup Elmer's glue
- 1 ½ cups shaving cream
- 2 ½ tablespoons contact solution

Option 3 (the one used for the recipe)

- 1/3 cup Elmer's white glue
- ½ teaspoon baking soda
- ¼ cup water
- 2-3 cups shaving cream (not shaving gel)
- 1.5 tablespoons contact solution
- Food coloring (to your preference)

Instructions:

- Add white glue to your bowl.
- Add in your water and baking soda and mix well.
- Then add in your shaving cream and mix again. Once that is mixed add in your food coloring until you are satisfied with the color.
- Now, slowly add in your contact solution a little bit at a time. Add in 1 tablespoon and knead for 5 minutes. Then add in the ½ tablespoon after.
- If it is still too sticky, then add in a few more drops of your contact solution until it is the desired consistency.

**You can add baby oil or lotion to your hands to help with the stickiness.

No Glue Dish Soap Slime

Ingredients:

- ½ cup cornstarch

- 1/4 cup dish soap

- 2-4 tablespoons oil

- Glitter

- Food coloring

Instructions:

- Begin by pouring the cornstarch into a large bowl or container.

- Slowly pour the dish soap into the bowl of cornstarch and mix.

- Keep mixing until you reach the desired consistency. It may require some elbow grease, and the process is a bit messy, but it will be worth it. Just keep mixing.

- Once the slime begins to form, remove it from the bowl and continue to knead it with clean, dry hands.

- If the slime is still too sticky, add a bit of cornstarch and mix it in.

- Then you should have your dish soap slime!

Unicorn Slime

Ingredients:

- 1 cup white school glue

- Liquid starch

- Food coloring (any pastel colors)

Instructions:

- First, pour 1 cup of glue into a bowl.

- Then add in your food coloring (the white glue will create pastel colors) and stir.

- Now add in your liquid starch and stir. You will immediately see the slime form. Continue stirring for a minute or so and then start kneading with your hands.

- Then, if you made multiple colors, you can twist them together to create your unicorn slime.

Glitter Slime

Ingredients:

- ¼ cup glitter glue or clear glue

- ½ tablespoon baking soda

- 1-2 teaspoons glitter

- 2-4 drops of food coloring (whatever color you desire)

- 1 teaspoon contact solution

- 1-2 drops of essential oils (if you desire)

Instructions:

- Add glue to a small bowl or container.

- Next, add your baking soda.

- Then add in as much glitter as you want.

- Add in your food coloring and essential oils if you desire.

- Next, add in your contact solution. Mix in slowly and add more if you need to.

**This needs to be mixed QUICKLY!

- Once the mixture starts to form, start to knead your slime. If you used a dark food coloring, you might want to start with a stir stick, because your hands will get stained. Work the slime until it is pliable.

- You will know when the slime is done because of the texture.

Edible Sugar Slime

Ingredients:

- 1 cup powdered sugar (a heaping cup)

- ¼ cup flour (also a heaping cup)

- 1-3 tablespoons oil (olive oil or any that you have on hand will do)

- Sprinkles (optional)

Instructions:

- Mix in your dry ingredients.

- Put a hole in the middle of them and add the oil, stirring until mixed.

- Once it is all mixed, take it out of the bowl and start kneading it on the counter.

- Mix in more oil as needed to get the stretchy consistency that you desire (it will be a little doughy).

- Finally, add sprinkles if you desire.

Glow in the Dark Slime

**There are different glow in the dark glues that you can use for this. Blue doesn't get as vibrant in the dark as green. The yellowish green is the "natural" glow in the dark color and is the most vibrant in the dark. Pink is more vibrant than blue, but is still less vibrant than green with the lights turned off.

**I would also recommend buying two bottles of the glue because they are 5 ounces each and I made mine with 6 ounces.

Ingredients:

- 1 bottle or 6 ounces glow in the dark glue

- ¼ tablespoon baking soda

- 2 tablespoons water

- 1 tablespoon contact solution

Instructions:

- Mix all of your slime ingredients into your bowl, except the glue.

- Then, you can mix your entire bottle of glow in the dark glue into the bowl. Make sure it is all out of the bottle or you will be left with a smaller batch of slime, or double the recipe.

**TIP: you can pour your water (2 tablespoons) into the glue bottle to get the extra glue out.

- Add your ¼ tablespoon of baking soda and 2 tablespoons of the water (if you have not already) into the bowl and mix thoroughly. If you want a more stretchy slime, you can add a little more water to your mix (up to ¼ cup total).

- Slowly add in your contact solution. Add in ½ tablespoon and stir, and then another ½ tablespoon and stir. You don't want to add too much, but if it is still sticky you can add a few more drops in.

- Once that is done, you can take the slime out of the bowl and start kneading it on your counter. It may still be sticky at this point, but that's okay. Just keep kneading until it is not sticky anymore.

- Now, as with any glow in the dark substance, you need to "charge" it. You can leave it out in a sunny area, or under a light. Make sure to spread it out so that it's all exposed. If it isn't, then certain areas may not glow.

Clear Water Slime

Ingredients:

- 3.4 ounces clear glue

- 7 ounces water

- 1 ounce contact solution

- .2 ounces baking soda

Instructions:

- Put the clear glue (100ml) into your mixing bowl and add about 60ml of water. Stir the mixture using your spoon until the glue mixes completely with the water.

- Add the contact lens solution to the mixture.

- Use a spoon to stir the mixture until you get an even consistency and a clear solution. Make sure that all the glue bubbles disappear from the mixture.

- Set the mixture aside. Take another bowl and put the baking soda in it.

- Add 200ml of hot water to the baking soda and stir until the powder melts completely, giving another clear solution.

- Next, allow the baking powder solution to cool off.

- When the solution has cooled, gently pour the glue mixture into the clear baking soda solution.

- Using your hands, try to stir the contents of the bowl gently.

- Remove or drain the baking soda solution, and leave the residue in the bowl.

- Allow the residue to air dry for a few minutes.

Shampoo Slime

Ingredients:

- ½ cup clear shampoo (or mostly clear)

- 1 teaspoon sugar (might need a little more)

- Bowl

**This will be cold. If you hold it in your hands for too long your fingers may start to tingle.

Instructions:

- Pour half a cup of shampoo into your bowl. You can use more shampoo, but it will take longer to develop.

- Add 1 teaspoon of sugar into the mix. The shampoo will start to thicken almost right away.

- Add a bit more sugar to the mix until the mixture clings to the spoon like wet slime would.

- Without glue, you will need to place the slime in the freezer for about 2 hours to finish it. The slime will thicken, but because of the ingredients in shampoo, it will not crystallize.

More Advanced and Different Ingredient Slimes

Floam Slime

Ingredients:

Option 1

- ½ cup clear glue
- ½ cup liquid starch
- Mini foam balls
- ½ cup warm water

Option 2

- 1 bottle of Elmer's glue (6 ounces) (glitter glue is always fun here)
- ½ teaspoon baking soda
- 1 ½ tablespoons contact solution
- Foam beads

Instructions:

**Note: if you want to make this floam slime more like slime and less like traditional floam, you can add 3 tablespoons of water to your slime before adding in the foam beads.

- Get a bowl to mix all of your ingredients in.
- Then add in one bottle of Elmer's glue.
- Add ½ teaspoon of baking soda into your bowl and mix thoroughly.
- Now you can add in your contact solution. Add in a ½ tablespoon to start and mix in. Then you can add another ½ tablespoon and mix well again. For the rest, add in slowly. Remember, you cannot take out ingredients, you can only put them in, and you don't want your slime to be too hard. Add the rest in slowly until you reach your desired consistency.
- Start kneading your slime once all of your contact solution is in. This may take 5 minutes or so. If it is too sticky, as mentioned before, put some baby oil or lotion on your hands and knead away. If that does not work, add a few more drops of contact solution to your slime.
- Your slime will not be very stretchy without water but that's what you want for the floam slime. Once you add in the beads it will be almost a crunchy slime, rather than the traditional stretchy slime.
- Then, add in your foam beads. Mix the beads in slowly. As mentioned before, you can always take out. Keep kneading the beads into your slime a little bit at a time until you have the right amount for your slime. The more you add the less slime-y it will be.

Water Bead Slime

Ingredients:

- 2 bottles clear glue

- Water beads

- Liquid starch

- Mixing bowl

Instructions:

- To start out, make your water beads. For this, follow the instructions on the package to hydrate your water beads.

- Then pour two bottles of clear glue into your bowl.

- From there, slowly add in the liquid starch while stirring. Keep adding a little at a time until the mixture begins to stick together and congregate in the center of the bowl.

- Then, continue to stir and add in the liquid starch until the slime no longer sticks to your fingers when you touch it.

- By this point, your water beads should be fully hydrated. If not just wait a few more minutes. Once they are hydrated, add them to your slime and knead. Some may not stay in your mixture and that is okay. You do not want too many in your slime or it will be harder to play with.

- Once they are mixed in as much as can be, stretch, squeeze and play with your slime!

Galaxy Slime

Ingredients:

- 3 mixing bowls/containers

- 1 (6-ounce) bottle of black glitter glue

- 10-ounce bottle of clear glue, divided

- 1 ½ cups water, divided

- 1 ½ teaspoons baking soda, divided

- 3 tablespoons contact solution, divided

- Purple food coloring (or red and blue)

- Teal food coloring (or lots of blue and a little green and yellow)

- Pink, purple, gold, and teal glitter (any glitter will do)

- Star confetti (optional)

Instructions:

**This slime is a combination of multiple colors of slime and glitter. For this recipe you will make three separate slimes and combine them at the end.

Black Glitter Slime

- Pour the black glitter glue into the mixing bowl with ½ cup of water and ½ teaspoon of baking soda. Stir well to combine.

- Then add in 1 tablespoon of the contact solution and mix. You should see the slime start to form right away.

- It will be super sticky so continue to knead the slime with your hands.

- Once it is no longer sticky, set it aside and move on to the next color.

Purple Glitter Slime

- Combine a bottle of clear glue into your new mixing bowl, with ½ cup of water and purple food coloring (or red and blue).

- Then mix in your pink and purple glitter. Stir very well to combine. You can add as much glitter as you like; just make sure it all mixes in.

- Add more food coloring as needed to reach the desired shade of purple.

- Next, add ½ teaspoon of baking soda and stir well.

- Now, add in 1 tablespoon of saline solution, a little at a time, mixing well.

- Then you can start kneading with your hands. Set aside to start on your next color.

Teal Glitter Slime

- Repeat the same steps as the purple glitter slime, except make teal with your food coloring (lots of blue with a little green and yellow) and use teal and gold glitters.

FINALLY!

- Once the three colors are made, you can twist them all together for an awesome galaxy effect. The more you play with this, the more it changes colors!

Gummy Bear Slime

Ingredients:

- 1 cup gummy bears (try to match like colors)

- 2 tablespoons cornstarch

- 1 tablespoon powdered sugar

- ½ tablespoon oil (as needed)

Instructions:

**Adult supervision should be used here since this slime mixture will be very hot at times.

- Place gummy bears in a microwave-safe bowl and heat for 30 seconds. There should be no chunks of bears left.

- Stir well and let the mixture cool.

- Combine cornstarch and powdered sugar and place half on a clean surface.

- Pour the gummy bear mixture onto the cornstarch mixture and when it is cool enough to touch, knead in the remaining cornstarch mixture.

- It will be very sticky at first, but as you continue to knead, it will get less sticky.

- Once everything is all mixed in, knead in a bit of the oil to help make the slime more stretchy and elastic. You shouldn't need all of the oil.

**This slime can be reheated and used one more time, but it is intended for a single use.

Jell-O Slime

Ingredients:

- Mixing bowl

- 3-ounce box of sugar free Jell-O (sugar free makes the best slime and does not dye hands as badly)

- 1 cup cornstarch

- ½ cup warm water

- A cookie sheet or tray (anything to protect your surface from getting stained)

Instructions:

- In a mixing bowl, combine the cornstarch and the Jell-O packet. Mix them together evenly using a spoon.

- Slowly mix in the water, stirring the entire time. The mixture might become tough as you add the water, but do not add more water. The consistency at this point will be more like oobleck than slime. Continue to stir the entire ½ cup of water until it is evenly mixed. If you ABSOLUTELY need to add water, add a small drop or two at a time.

- Now you can start to knead your slime and play with it!

**If this is stored in an airtight container in the refrigerator, it can last for a week. However, you may need to add a drop of water here and there to bring it back to your desired consistency.

Edible Marshmallow Slime

Ingredients:

- 1 cup marshmallow fluff

- ¾ cup cornstarch

- ¼ cup powdered sugar

Instructions:

- Add the marshmallow fluff, powdered sugar, and ¼ cup of cornstarch to your mixing bowl.

- Stir together until all of the ingredients are mixed well.

- Add remaining ½ cup of cornstarch a little at a time and finish by kneading it by hand. If it is too sticky, add in 1 teaspoon of cornstarch at a time. You don't want too much.

**TIP: coat your hands with coconut oil (or another oil) before kneading to prevent the slime from sticking to your hands.

**If the slime gets thicker when you play with it, simply put it in the microwave for 5-10 seconds to soften.

Edible Chocolate Pudding Slime

Ingredients:

- 1 snack pack pudding cup

- 1 tablespoon cornstarch at a time

- Mixing bowl

- Sprinkles

Instructions:

- Put one of your pudding cups in your mixing bowl.

- Then add in 1 tablespoon of cornstarch at a time and mix. Continue adding 1 tablespoon of cornstarch until your slime forms.

- Once that is complete, sprinkle a little more cornstarch on your slime and take it out of your bowl and start to knead it with your hands.

- Once it is formed you can add sprinkles if you so desire.

Avalanche Slime (3-part instructions)

Instructions:

White Glue Slime

Ingredients:

- 1 cup white school glue

- ¼ - ½ cup water

- ½ teaspoon baking soda

- 3 tablespoons contact solution

Instructions:

- To start, add 1 cup of glue to a medium size mixing bowl.

- Add in your water and baking soda and stir to mix thoroughly. If you want to add any food coloring to your white glue slime, do so now.

- Finally, add in your contact solution and stir until you have your slime. Knead by hand and add in more contact solution if it is still too sticky.

Clear Glue Slime

Ingredients:

- ½ cup clear glue (with PVA)

- ½ cup water (to mix with glue)

- ½ cup hot tap water (to mix with borax powder)

- ¼ teaspoon borax powder

Instructions:

- In a bowl mix ½ cup water and ½ cup glue.

- Then mix ¼ teaspoon borax powder and ½ cup warm water in a separate bowl. Hot tap water is fine. Spend a minute stirring to make sure the borax powder is mixed very well.

- Add the borax mixture to the glue mixture and start stirring. Your slime should begin to form instantly. Keep stirring until your slime is completely formed and move to a clean and dry container. Do not worry about leftover liquid. That is okay.

- Start kneading your slime. It may be stringy at first, but just work that out and the consistency should change to make your final clear slime.

Avalanche

Ingredients:

- 1 batch of white slime (instructions are below)

- 1 batch of clear slime (instructions are below)

- 2 colors of food coloring

- 1 small container with lid

Instructions for the avalanche:

- To make the avalanche happen, you need to open up a small or medium container. The bigger container you have the longer the avalanche effect will take.

- Get your clear slime and add some color to it. Make sure you keep the color light.

- Now, put the colored slime on the sides of your container. Make sure it is pressed to the bottom of the container.

- Then top the clear glue slime with the white slime. Press down on the slime and put the lid on your container.

- Let it sit for 24 hours and it should mold together and make an avalanche effect. Then play away!

Magnetic Slime

Ingredients:

- 1 bottle of school glue

- 3 tablespoons magnetic powder (Amazon: black iron oxide)

- Up to 4 ounces liquid starch

- Neodymium magnets

Instructions:

**This can be a very messy recipe and may turn things black (hands and bowls), so be prepared for that.

- Combine the glue and the magnetic powder in a bowl and stir until completely mixed (you can use a craft stick to stir).

- Once combined, slowly add in small amounts of your liquid starch and mix well. Continue to add in the starch until you reach the desired consistency - between 2-4 ounces.

- After everything is mixed together, you can take the slime out of the bowl and see how it reacts to your magnets!

Chalkboard Slime

Ingredients:

- 4 ounces white glue
- 1 teaspoon baking soda
- ½ teaspoon contact solution
- 2 tablespoons chalkboard paint
- Chalk markers
- Mixing bowls

Instructions:

- Pour 4 ounces of your glue into a mixing bowl.

- Then, add 2 tablespoons of chalkboard paint to your glue and mix thoroughly.

- Add in 1 teaspoon of baking soda to the glue and paint mix. Then stir until completely combined.

- Next, add in ½ teaspoon of contact solution and stir. Your slime should begin to thicken. If the slime is too sticky, add in a few more drops of your contact solution. It should come away from the sides of the bowl.

- Finally take out and knead for a few minutes. This will fully combine all of the ingredients.

Draw on it

Now that your slime is made, you can draw on it using your chalkboard markers. If you press too hard it might pull the slime and not draw properly, so make dots to draw. Once you are done drawing, distort it. Pull the slime and watch your drawing elongate and change. To make a new drawing, simply knead the slime until the colors disappear and you can start again!

Take it a step further

If you would like to take a moment to teach your child even more, you can talk to them about the art of dot painting, called pointillism. Pointillism is a technique that was developed in the late 1800s by Georges Seurat and Paul Signac. This style of art involves using fine dots of color instead of brushstrokes. If you make these dots close enough and you stand back, your brain will actually connect the dots. It is a great optical trick.

Then you can talk about distortion, which is also used in the art world. After you create your drawing and are ready to start a new one, you can pull your slime apart slowly. This will cause your dots to stretch and turn into strips of color. You can use distortion to create the illusion of 3D space on a 2D surface.

Kinetic Sand Slime

Ingredients:

- 1 cup white glue

- 1/3 cup starch

- 1 cup fine grain sand

- 1 spoonful soap

- 1 spoonful cornstarch

Instructions:

- To start, put your sand in your mixing bowl.

- Then, add about a spoonful of cornstarch to your sand and mix until it is all blended together.

- Now, add in 1 spoonful of soap and stir again.

- Now it is time to make the slime portion. Add in your white glue and starch and stir everything together.

- Once it is absorbed you can start to knead your kinetic slime. Add more starch if needed. If you add too much, you will be left with a hard rock of sand.

Soft Clay Slime

Ingredients:

- ½ cup Elmer's white glue

- ½ teaspoon baking soda

- Food coloring

- 2 ounces soft modeling clay

- 1 tablespoon contact solution

Instructions:

- Add ½ cup of glue to your bowl.

- Mix with ½ cup of water.

- Then add your food coloring as desired.

- Stir in ½ teaspoon of baking soda.

- Then, mix in 1 tablespoon of contact solution and stir until slime forms and pulls away from the sides of the bowl. You may need to add more contact solution if your slime is still too sticky.

- Once your slime is made, you can start kneading in your soft clay. This will take a few minutes (and some strong hands) to work it in well.

**Clay notes: if your clay is dense, you should use less. Less dense clay requires you to use more. Feel free to experiment with different consistencies of clay.

You will usually use around 1/3 of the standard 4-ounce package of Crayola Model Magic Clay.

Start by softening up your clay. Then flatten it out and put it on top of your slime. Fold the mixture in by kneading and squishing it.

Heat-Sensitive Color-Changing Slime

Ingredients:

- ¼ cup white school glue

- 1 tablespoon water

- 3 teaspoons thermochromic pigment

- ¼ cup liquid starch

- Food coloring

Instructions:

- Decide on your color scheme. The color of the thermochromic pigment will be the color of the slime when it's cold. Then pick an alternating color of food coloring for the hot color.

  **Blue pigment with yellow food coloring turns slime teal and turns yellow when hot. Red pigment with yellow food coloring turns slime an orange-red color and yellow when hot. Blue pigment with red food coloring turns the slime purple and then pink when it's hot.

- Pour the ¼ cup of glue into a large bowl. Then add in 1 tablespoon of water and stir until it is all combined. Add in your food coloring and mix well. Then add in 3 teaspoons of your thermochromic pigment and mix until it is evenly distributed.

- Add 1/8 cup of liquid starch and mix until it's thick and slimy. Then knead the slime with your hands. Add the remaining 1/8 cup of liquid starch. This step is important because you don't want any glue left in the middle of your slime.

- If the slime is still sticky add in a little more starch and knead until it is not.

Fish Bowl Slime

Ingredients:

- ½ cup clear or white school glue

- 1 tablespoon contact solution

- ½ cup water

- ¼ to ½ teaspoon baking soda

- Food coloring

- 1/3 cup fishbowl beads

Instructions:

- In a bowl, completely mix in ½ cup of water and ½ cup glue.

- Then, add the food coloring. It will be lighter if you use the white glue, but use clear for the jewel tone colors.

- Stir in the ¼ to ½ teaspoon of baking soda and mix well. You can play around with to get the desired firmness.

- Next, add in the fishbowl beads and stir. Do not add too many or they will make your slime brittle and it will not have the stretch you desire and love. Plus, some beads might fall out.

- Then, add in your activator. Mix the 1 tablespoon of contact solution and stir until the slime forms and pulls away from the sides of your bowl. If the slime is still too sticky, add a few more drops of the contact solution and knead it some more.

- Finally, have fun with your slime!

Slushie Slime

Ingredients:

- 1 airtight container
- 1 bottle of clear glue
- ½ cup water
- ½ teaspoon baking soda
- 1 tablespoon contact solution
- Food coloring
- Slushie beads
- Small bowl

Instructions:

- Pour the entire 5-ounce bottle of clear glue into your bowl.
- Then, add in ½ cup of water and mix together.
- Next, add in ½ teaspoon of baking soda and stir together.
- Once that is complete, add in the 1 tablespoon of contact solution and your mixture will begin to form instantly.
- Then you can drop in your red food coloring and mix. It is best to do at least 5 drops.
- Next, add in the slushie beads. This mixture will be very sticky still so do not panic! Just keep mixing the solution in your bowl until it starts to form. Then knead until the slime is no longer sticky.

**After a while the beads will either rise to the top or settle to the bottom. This is normal, just mix it all back up when you go to play with it.

Nail Polish Slime

Ingredients:

- Glass mixing bowl (DO NOT USE PLASTIC OR STYROFOAM)

- 3 bottles of nail polish

- 1 cup clear glue

- 1 teaspoon baking soda

- ½ teaspoon contact solution (might need more)

Instructions:

- To start, pour 1 cup of your clear glue into your glass mixing bowl.

- Then, pour in your 3 bottles of nail polish and mix with the glue. Try to get all of the nail polish out of the bottles. The results are worth it!

- Mix until it is all combined.

- Next, add in your 1 teaspoon of baking soda and mix.

- Now, it is time for your contact solution. Mix in your ½ teaspoon of contact solution. You might need more depending on how sticky your mixture is.

- Once your slime is formed, you can remove it from your bowl and knead it. If it is still too sticky you can always use more contact solution. Just do not use too much.

- After kneading, you will be left with vibrant nail polish slime!

Scented Slimes

Scented slimes not only smell good, they can also be relaxing for anyone who uses and plays with them. This can help with anxiety or falling asleep. The possibilities and scents are endless. Just grab your essential oils and go to town. Essential oils can also be added to any slime mixture. You can make scents fruity, like candy, or anything else you can imagine. Go wild!

Pineapple Scented Slime

Ingredients:

- ½ cup water

- 1 tablespoon pineapple Jell-O powder

- ½ cup clear glue

- ½ to ¾ cup liquid starch

- Yellow food coloring (optional)

Instructions:

- Pour your water and Jell-O into a mixing bowl and stir until the Jell-O starts to dissolve.

- Then stir in ½ cup of clear glue. If you want to add in food coloring, you can do so now. The Jell-O will give your slime a tint of yellow, but if you would like it more vibrant you can add in more yellow.

- Now, to add in your activator. Start by adding in ½ cup of liquid starch. If you need to add more you can do so in small increments until it is no longer sticky.

- Finish up by kneading your slime with your hands.

Essential Oil Slime

Ingredients:

- 1 bottle of glue (clear or white)

- ½ teaspoon baking soda

- Food coloring of your choice

- Essential oil drops (your preference)

- 2 teaspoons of contact solution (might need more)

- ½ teaspoon oil (your choice)

Instructions:

- Grab your mixing bowl and pour in your bottle of glue.

- Next, mix in your ½ teaspoon of baking soda.

- At this point you can mix in your food coloring. Make it whatever color you want!

- Add in your Essential oils until you are happy with the smell and you can smell it when playing with it. Mix until it is all blended in.

- Finally add in your contact solution and mix until your slime pulls away from the edges of your bowl. Then you can take it out of the bowl and start kneading it.

- If your scent is over powering then add in your oil to tone it down a bit. This will also help with the stickiness.

Alternatives to Slime

Slime is fun, but so are these slime alternatives that you can play around with. These are like slime in the sense that each recipe is unique and you can make them your own as well. Have fun!

Oobleck

This substance is a non-Newtonian fluid, just like slime. What this means is that oobleck is a substance that can mimic the qualities of a liquid and a solid. The viscosity of this liquid changes depending on what you are doing with it. Examples of Newtonian fluids are water and gasoline; they do not change. Examples of non-Newtonian fluids, other than oobleck, are ketchup and silly putty.

Ingredients:

- 1 part water

- 1.5 parts cornstarch

- Food coloring (if you desire)

- Mixing bowl

Instructions:

- Mix these all together until your oobleck is consistent.

**When making this with children, take the opportunity to teach them about solids and liquids. Notice how hard the oobleck feels when you tap or hit it. Ask your child why they think it becomes a solid when pressure is applied. Next, let the oobleck sit in a glass bowl (the one you mix it in is fine, even if it is not glass or clear). Observe how the liquid and solid separate. Talk to them about how this is because it is a suspension and not an actual mixture. Now it is time to mix your oobleck. Stir it with a spoon. Predict and observe how long it will take before you cannot stir any longer.

**Do not put this in your garbage disposal when you're finished with it. Throw it in the trash in a bag. It is too thick and may cause a blockage.

Silly Putty

Originally named "nutty putty," this is a substance that will stretch, bounce, and even shatter if hit with enough force. Silly Putty will also pick up a perfect copy of a printed image when you flatten it against something like a newspaper or a comic. There are a few different ways to make Silly Putty.

Option 1

Ingredients:

- 1 cup cornstarch
- ½-1 cup gel soap (Method brand soap works great)
- Food coloring
- Mixing bowl

Instructions:

- To start, mix the cornstarch and soap into your bowl.
- If you would like food coloring, add that now. It will stain your hands if you use too much all at once, so start out slow and work it in.
- Start by mixing with a spoon, and once it starts to get crumbly, start kneading it with your hands.
- Once your putty is moldable and not sticking to your fingers, it's ready to go! It may be a little slimy, but that's normal.

Option 2

Ingredients:

- ¼ teaspoon borax powder
- ¼ cup white glue
- ¼ cup water
- Food coloring
- Bowl
- Measuring cups

Instructions:

- To start, put your ¼ cup of glue into your bowl.

- Then add the desired amount of food coloring.

- Next, mix in your borax powder (note: this is your slime activator).

- Add in ¼ teaspoon of borax to ¼ cup of water, stir, and then mix with your glue solution. Your solution will come together almost instantly.

- Keep stirring. It will become more difficult so you will want to use your hands and knead until it is smooth like silly putty.

Option 3

Ingredients:

- 1 cup cornstarch

- 3-4 ounces lotion (scented or unscented depending on your preference)

- Food coloring (optional)

- Essential oils (optional)

Instructions:

- Start by putting 1 cup of cornstarch in your bowl.

- Then squeeze in 3-4 ounces of lotion onto your cornstarch and mix together with a spoon.

- Once you are able to and the mixture is less messy, you can start to knead it with your hands until the dough is smooth.

- Finally, add in your color and essential oils if you desire.

**This silly putty might be a different consistency because of the lotion. If it is too sticky, add a little more cornstarch. If it is too doughy, add a little more lotion. This is all to your preference.

**Keep in an airtight container for long-term use.

Playdough

This is a dough-like product that is usually composed of flour, water, salt, borax, and mineral oil. Children can use it for arts and crafts or to just have fun with. It was originally intended to be wallpaper cleaner in the 1930s. Here are a couple options for making your own Playdough and saving money in the process.

Option 1

Ingredients:

- 1 cup flour

- ½ cup salt

- 2 tablespoons cream of tartar

- 1 tablespoon oil

- 1 cup water

- Food coloring

Instructions:

- First, you will mix the flour, salt, cream of tartar and oil into a pan.

- Next, add the water and mix well.

- Now you will need to cook the mixture over medium heat for 3-5 minutes. Stir this constantly until the mixture becomes firm.

- Once it is firm you can remove it from the pan and knead it until it is soft.

- Then add in your food coloring until it is all mixed in and enjoy!

Option 2

Ingredients:

- 2 cups cornstarch

- 1 cup hair conditioner

- Food coloring

Instructions:

This recipe for Playdough is the most simple.

- For this you just need to put the cornstarch into a large bowl.

- Then mix in the hair conditioner. You can use your hands or a spoon for this. It will start coming together quickly and be very pliable and smooth.

- At this point, you can add in your food coloring to make the desired color or colors.

- Depending on your consistency, you may need to add in a little more hair conditioner, but do this a little at a time.

**Do not use expensive conditioner for this. The conditioners smell good and make your hands soft as you play. Use conditioners that you or your children like.

**Keep in an airtight container or Ziploc bag when not in use.

Other Things to do With Slime

Besides playing with slime and teaching your children the science behind it, you can use slime to clean dust and small items off of most surfaces. This will make your slime unusable for future playing, but it can get to hard to reach places.

Resources and Suppliers

Materials

Look to your local grocery stores for materials to make your slime products.

Glue: You don't need anything fancy. Elmer's glue will work just as well as the store brand glue. Just make sure it has the PVA in it. Most Targets and Walmarts also carry the glitter glue.

Contact solution: This is the same as your glue. You do not have to buy anything fancy. As long as it contains boric acid you are good to go.

Baking soda and cornstarch: These ingredients can be found in your baking aisle. Most people even have them handy at home. It doesn't matter what brand you buy.

Borax and liquid starch: These can usually be found in the laundry aisle. Just make sure your borax is in powder form. If you cannot find liquid starch, Amazon has some in bulk for pretty cheap.

Food coloring: Use what you have. If you do not have any, look at your local grocery store in the baking aisle. Here you can find all sorts of colors. You only need the four main colors for slime, but if you want to spend the extra money, then you can get other colors as well.

Water: Why go fancy? That is just not necessary. Use your tap water to make the perfect slime.

Shaving cream: This is another ingredient that you may have lying around your house. If not, most stores and even gas stations sell cans of shaving cream. Just make sure you get cream and not gel.

Ziploc bags: Any type of Ziploc bag will work. You can find these at almost any store that you shop at. The amount of slime you are going to make and the size of your batches will determine the size and number of bags you need.

Airtight containers: Most containers are airtight; just make sure they are not too large.

**If you cannot find some of the special ingredients, you may need to look online or at a craft store. Here are some great resources for that:

Amazon: Here you can find almost anything you could ever need for slime. They also carry a lot of it in bulk, so if you know you are going to be making a lot of slime, it will be cheaper to go this route.

Hobby Lobby or your local craft stores: These places will also carry your extra supply needs, like glitters, glues, foam beads, and much more.

Sam's Club or other bulk stores: If you are planning on making a lot of slime and want to have these items in bulk, you can buy them at stores like Sam's Club as well. This way, you won't have to keep buying products over and over again.

Conclusion

Slime is unique no matter how you make it, whether you are following the instructions as written, or doing it the way someone else did. Science can be tricky and each person might get a slightly different result.

Let your imagination run wild. Just because there are recipes here does not mean you have to follow them to the letter. Experiment with different ratios, use new and exciting additives, and never be scared to mess up and start over. That is what science is all about. It is about learning and creating something new and exciting for everyone.

If you've enjoyed reading this book, subscribe* to my mailing list for exclusive content and sneak peaks of my future books.

Visit the link below:

http://eepurl.com/dCTyG1

OR

Use the QR Code:

(*Must be 13 years or older to subscribe)

Made in the USA
Las Vegas, NV
17 June 2022

50342844R00036